D. S. Publishers (India)
the Bookmaster
DELHI

Language Skills

Pre-Primary Learning Skills
B
Crayon

Key Words

Shab

This book belongs to

____

____

D. S. Publishers (India)

First Published 2001
22nd Reprint 2022

ISBN 978-81-87131-64-9

Published by
DS Publishers (India)
7/7 Ansari Road, Daryaganj
New Delhi 110 002
+91 11 4156 3757
info@dspublishers.com
www.dspublishers.com

Type-setting and Cover Design by
Lovika Arts

Printed at
Balaji Offset

₹ 135

PREFACE

Children of the ages between 3 years and 5 years are at the Pre-Primary stage of learning, and just about awakened to their sensory skills.

This series of books is basically revolving round children of these ages — and are thus directed towards the development of the skills to which the tiny beings are getting introduced to. They are being initiated into the concepts that are necessary for further progress of the learning procedures.

This set of books deals separately with specific language skills. With these books at hand, followed by the guidance of the teacher or parents will take the children ahead in fixing in their minds the correct concepts necessary for further education.

The activities enshrined in these books help the child in developing his/her basic skills of reading and writing.

Colours

Read and colour.

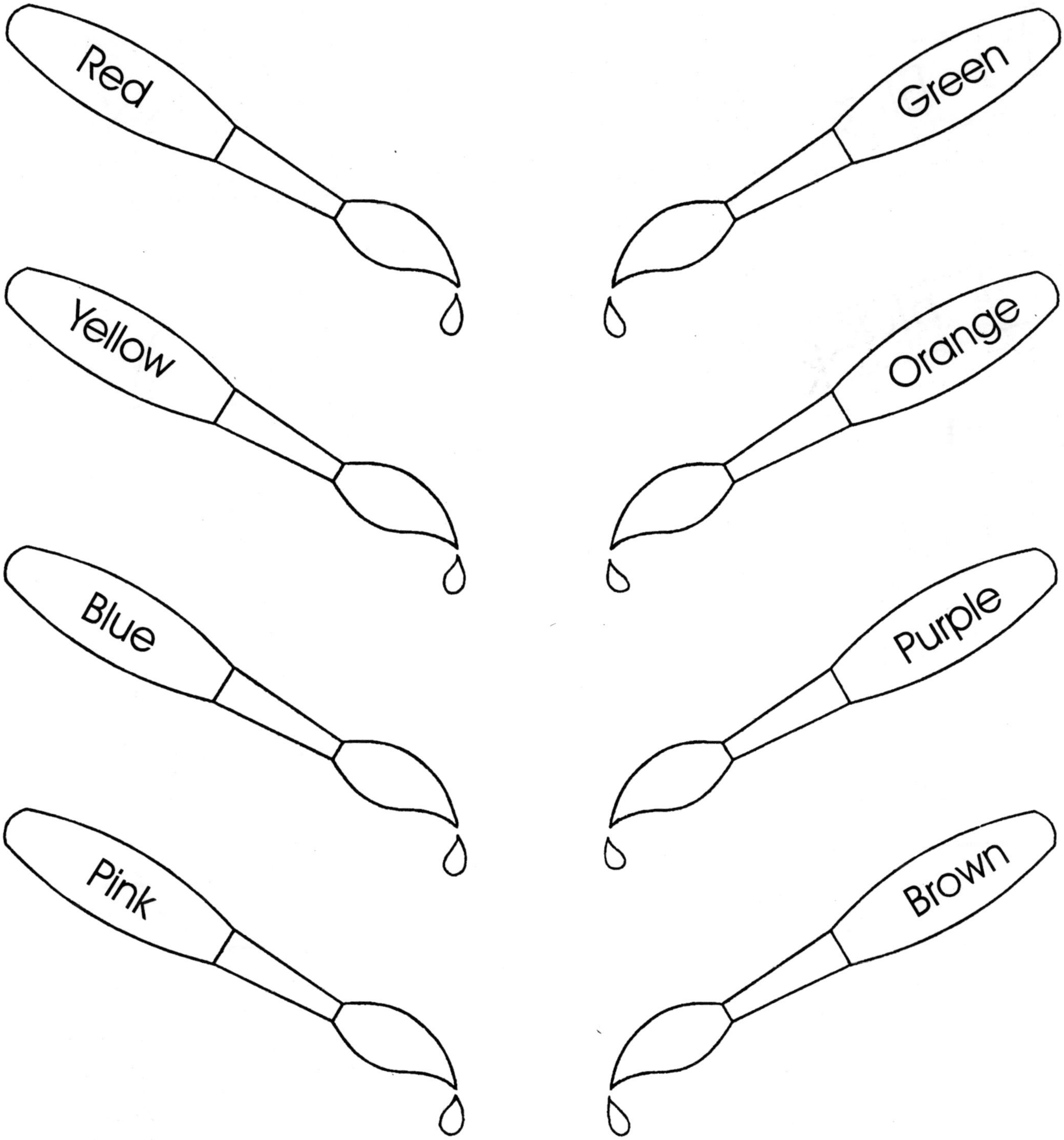

Teacher/Parents : Read each word aloud. Help the child to colour the brushes accordingly.

Colours

Trace the words with crayons and match.

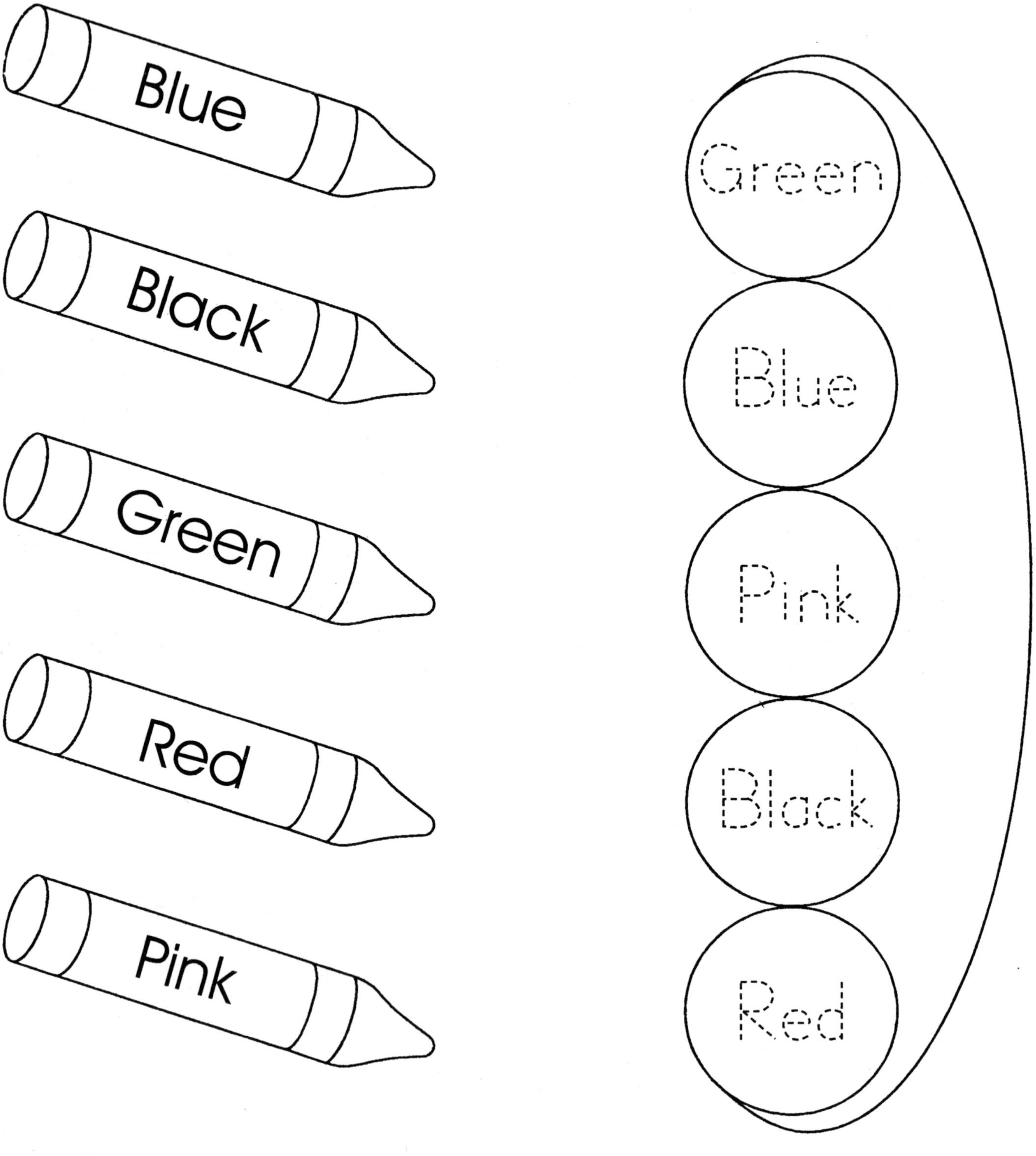

Teacher/Parents : Help the child to recognise the colour words.

Colours

Draw lines to join the pictures with the correct words.

yellow sun

pink rose

brown dog

brown
pink
green
white
yellow
black

white rabbit

black shoes

green leaves

Teacher/Parents : Read the names of object words aloud. Help the child to match the colour words with objects.

Fruits

Draw lines to match the names of the fruits. Colour the fruits.

mango

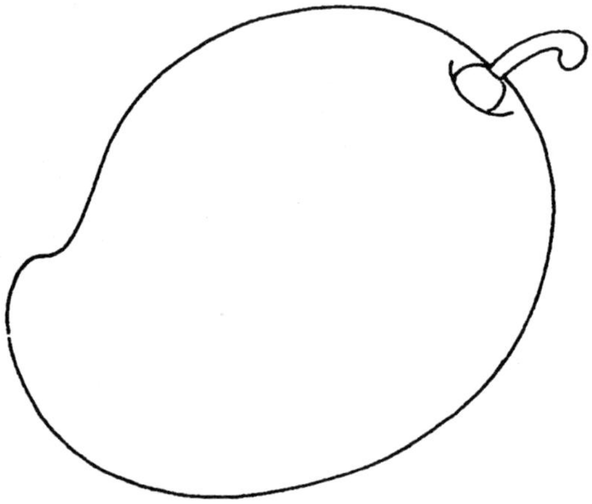

orange

apple

Teacher/Parents : Read the names of the fruits. Direct the child in colouring the fruits.

Fruits

Colour the fruits. Match the pictures with words.

grapes

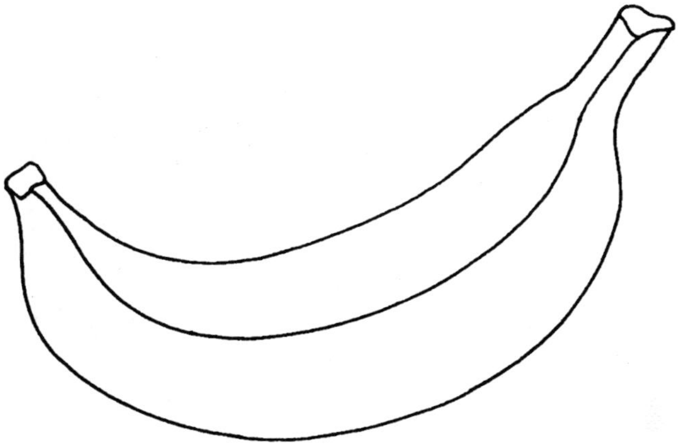

pear

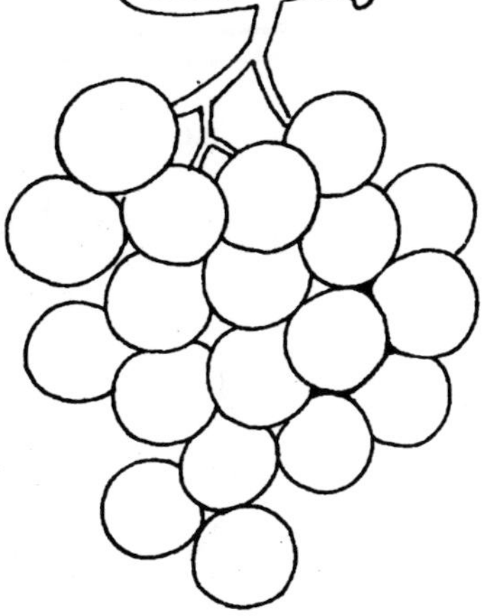

banana

Teacher/Parents : Help the child to recognise the fruits.

Fruits

Put a tick ☑ to the word which belongs to the picture.

	grass
	grapes
	green

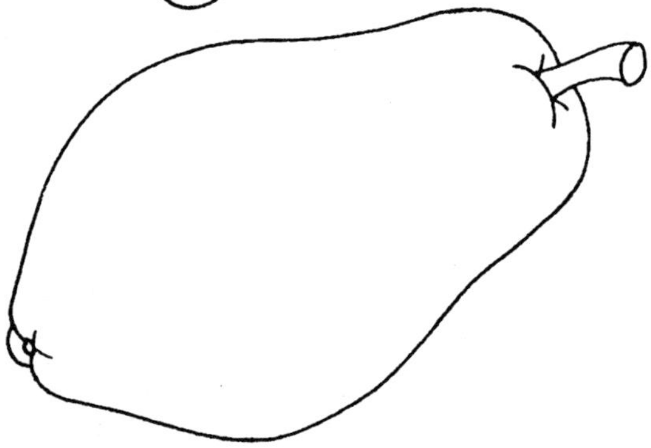

	papaya
	peas
	potato

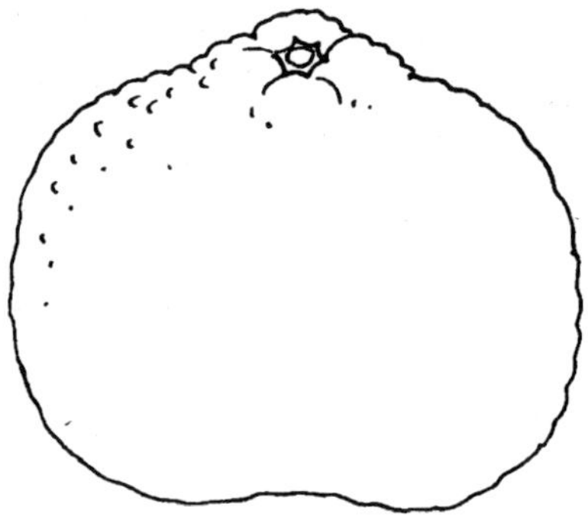

	onion
	orchid
	orange

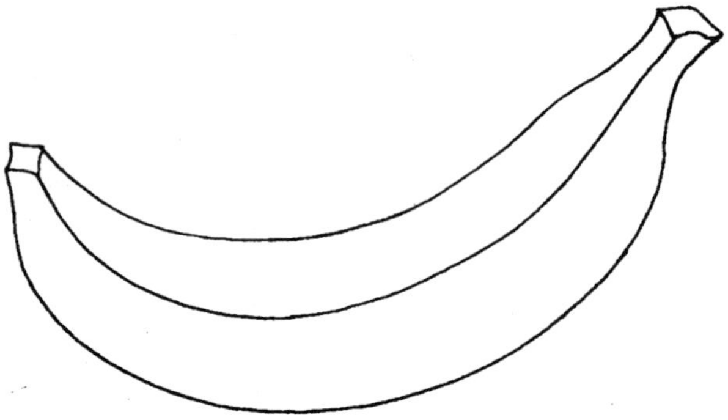

	banana
	brinjal
	beans

Teacher/Parents : Ask the child to read the words aloud.

Fruits

Put a tick ☑ to the correct word which belongs to the picture.

	peanut
	pear
	papaya

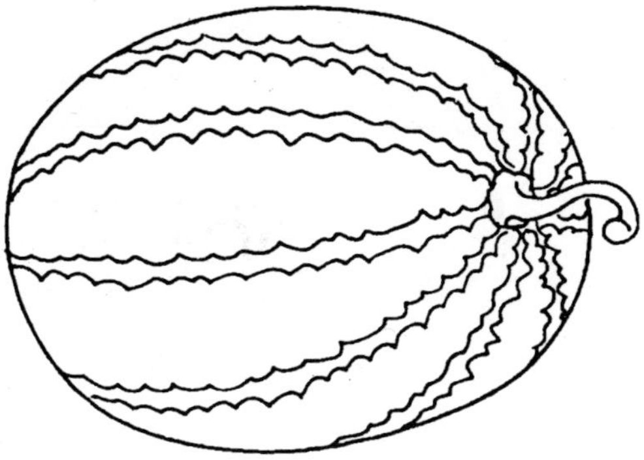

	water
	watch
	watermelon

	axe
	apple
	ant

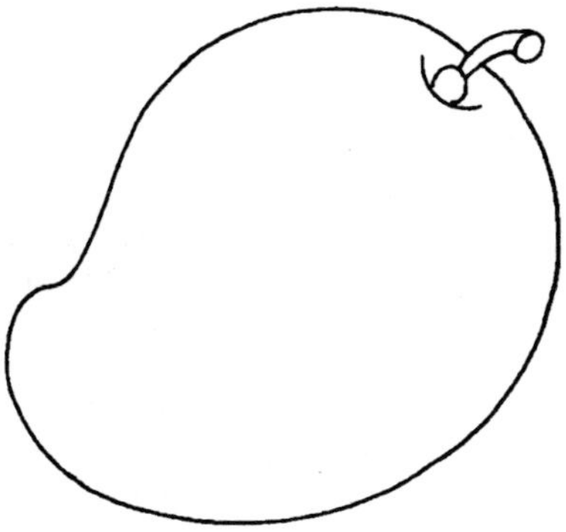

	mango
	moon
	money

Vegetables

Draw lines to join the correct words with the pictures. Colour the vegetables.

cauliflower

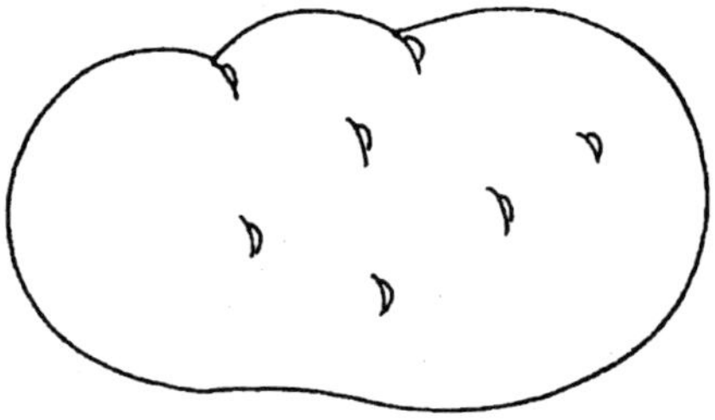

onion

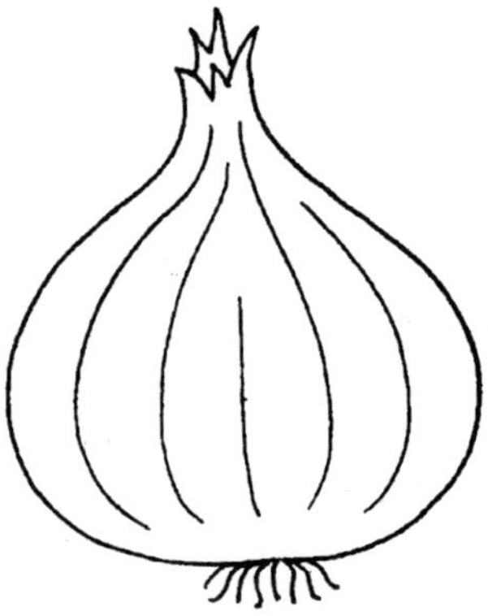

tomato

potato

Teacher/Parents : Help the child to identify the vegetables.

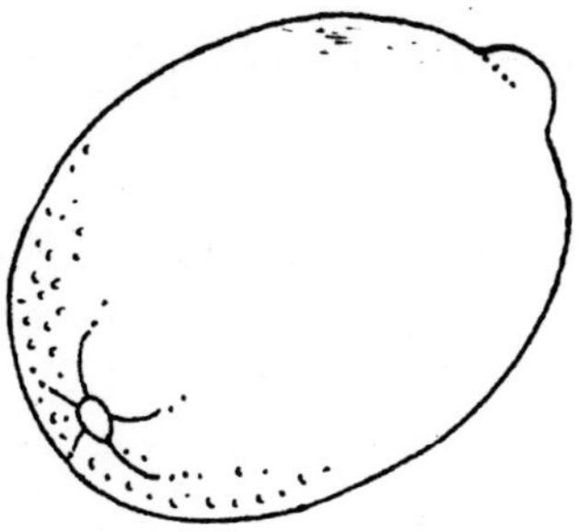

beans

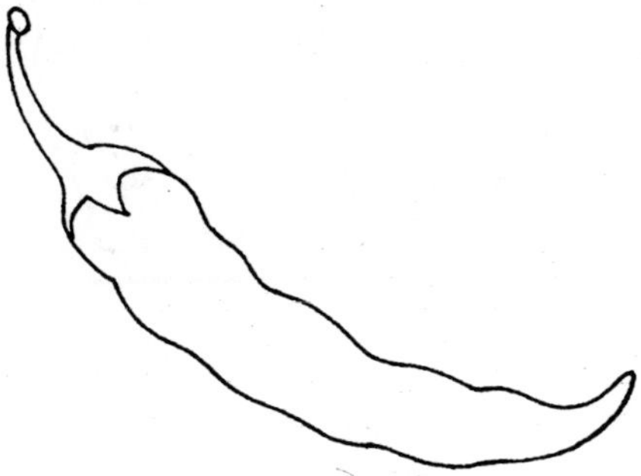

brinjal

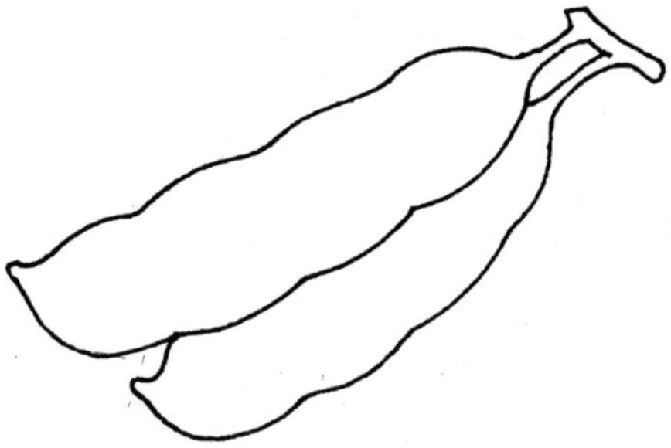

chilli

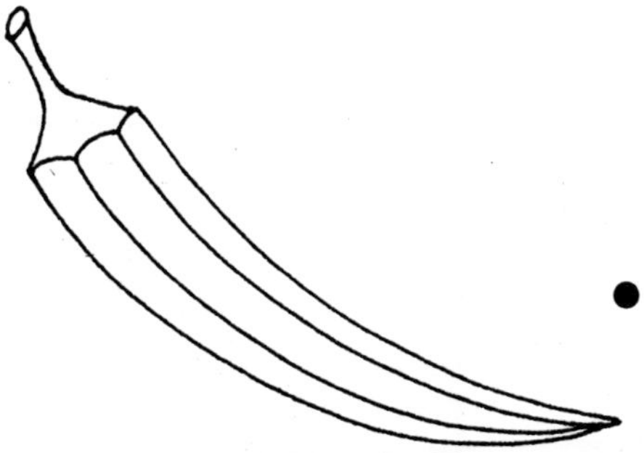

lemon

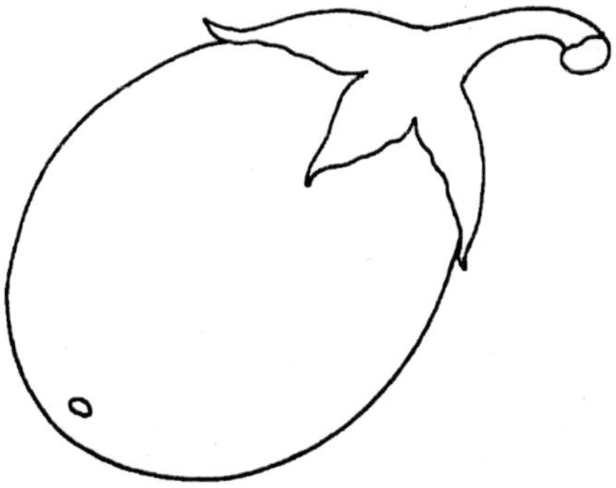

ladyfinger

Vegetables

Read the word and circle the correct picture.

onion	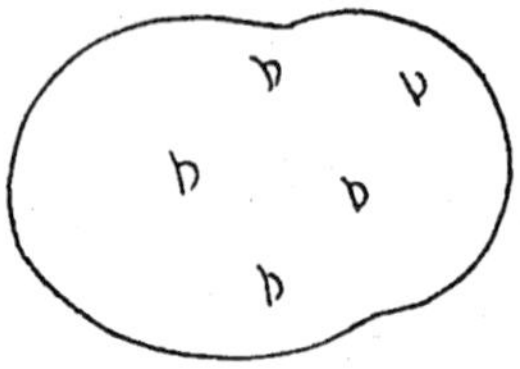		
cauliflower			
tomato	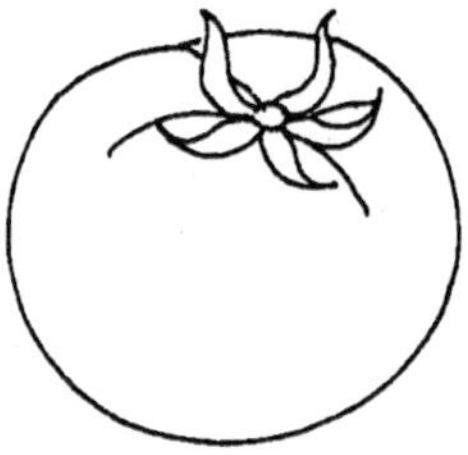	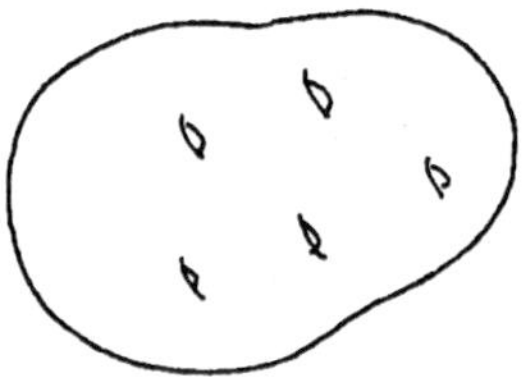	
ladyfinger	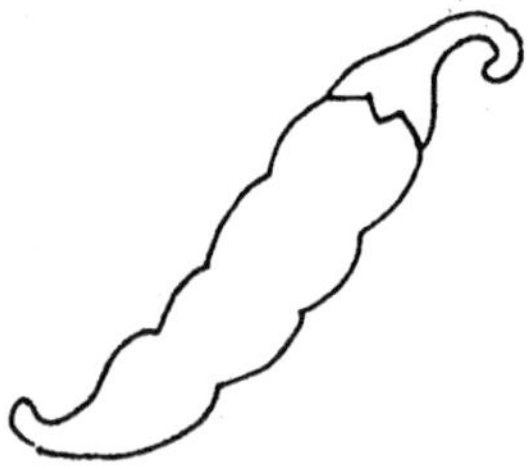	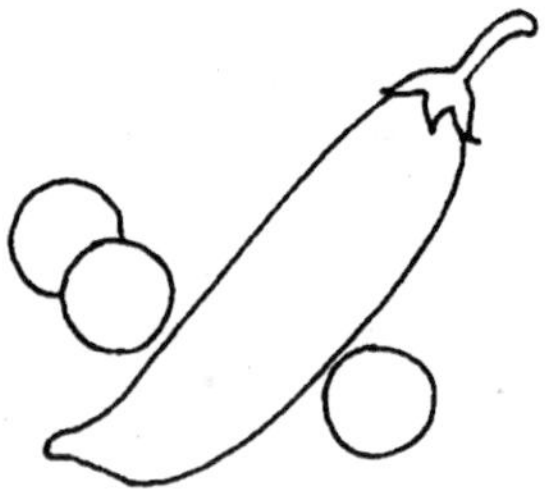	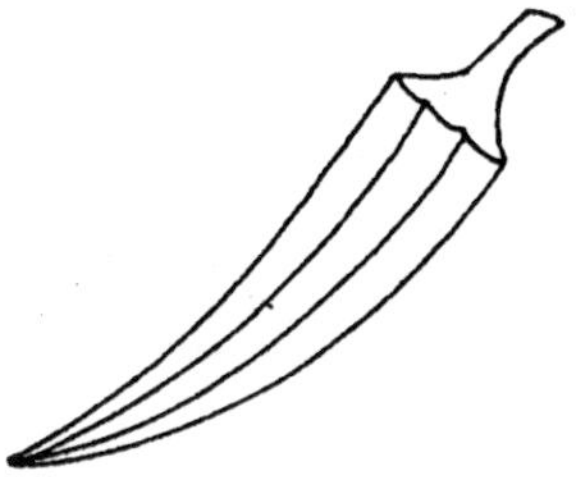
peanuts	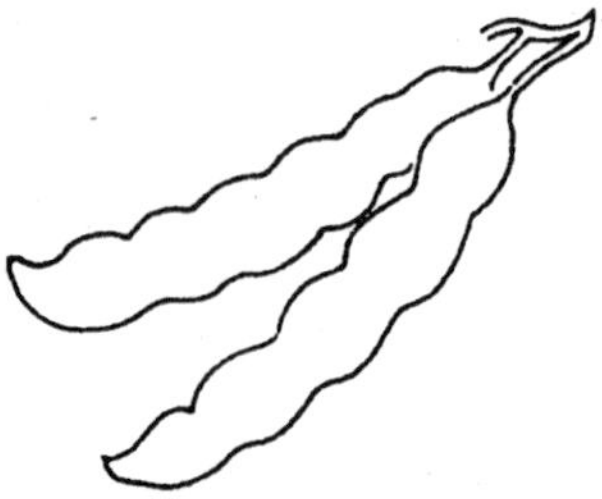		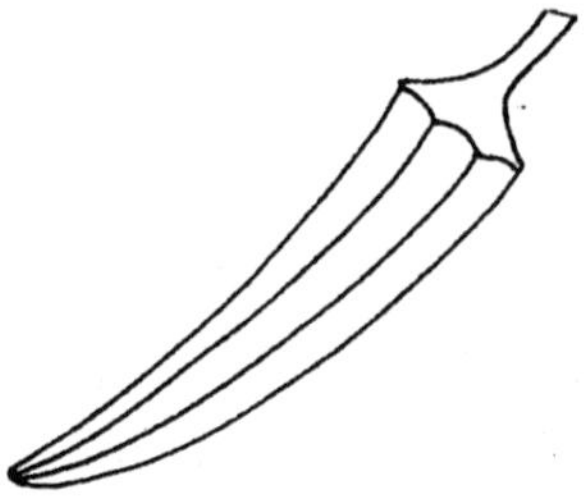

Teacher/Parents : Ask the child to read aloud the word and then identify the picture that matches.

Vegetables

Put a tick ☑ in the box of the correct picture.

brinjal	 ☐	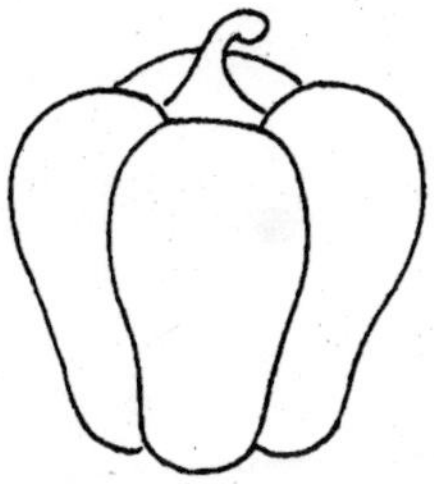 ☐	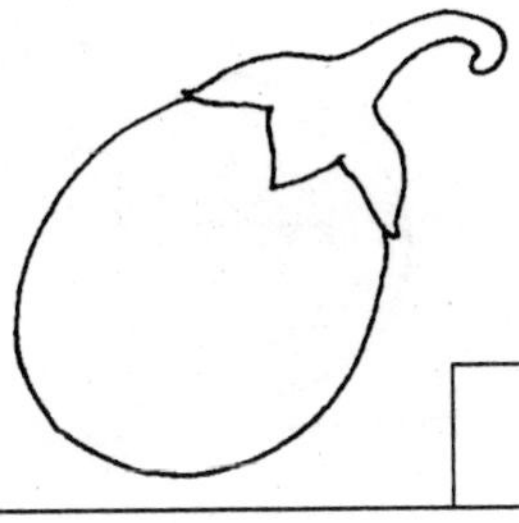 ☐
Bottle-gaurd	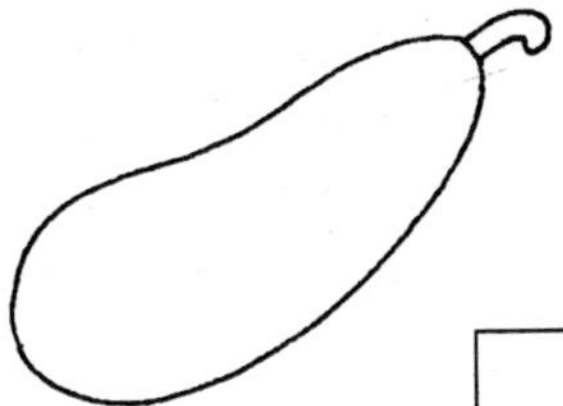 ☐	 ☐	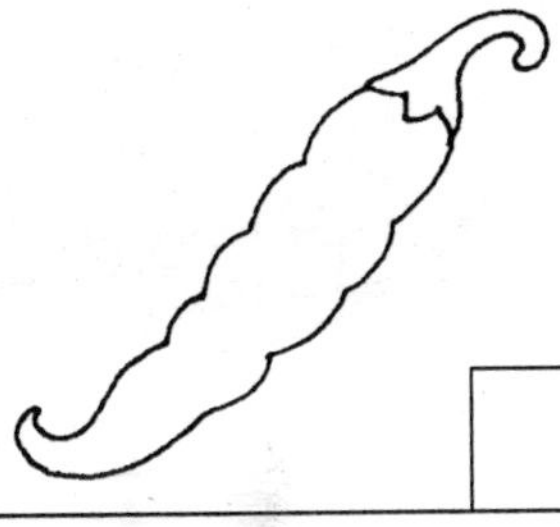 ☐
capsicum	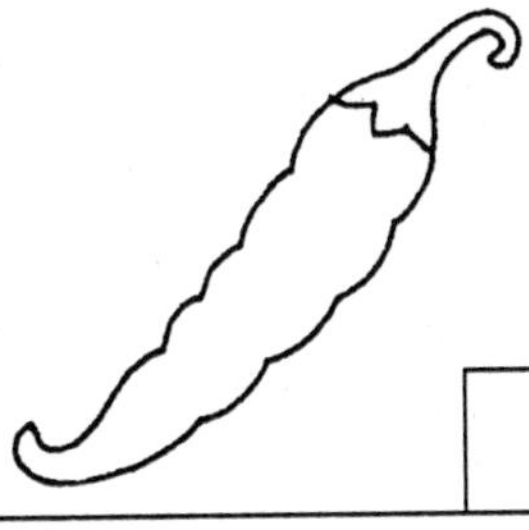 ☐	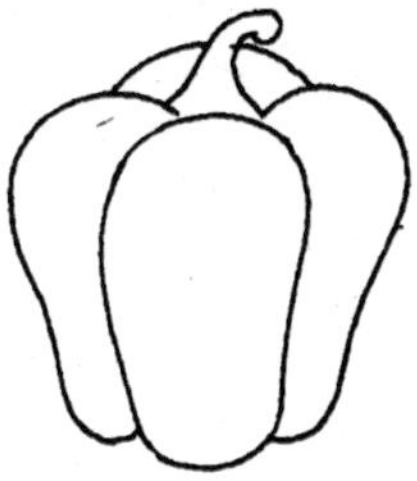 ☐	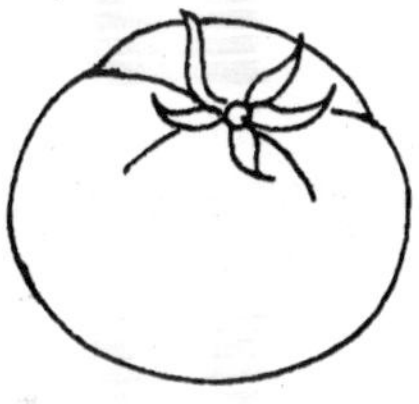 ☐
cabbage	 ☐	 ☐	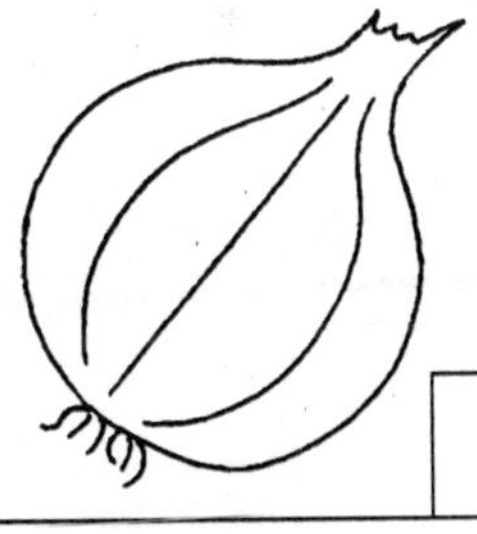 ☐
potato	 ☐	 ☐	 ☐

Draw lines to match the pictures with the correct words.

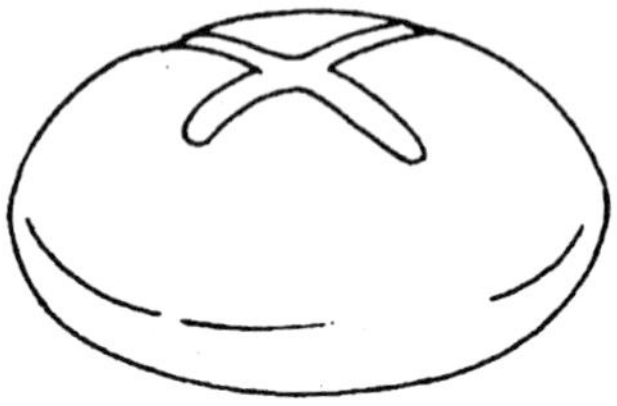 • • fish

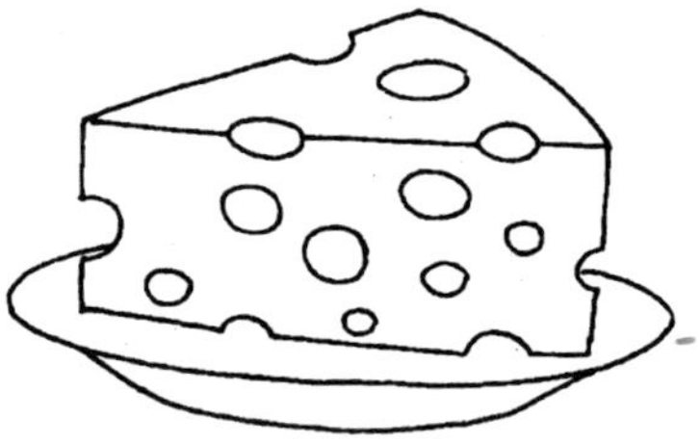 • • soup

• • cheese

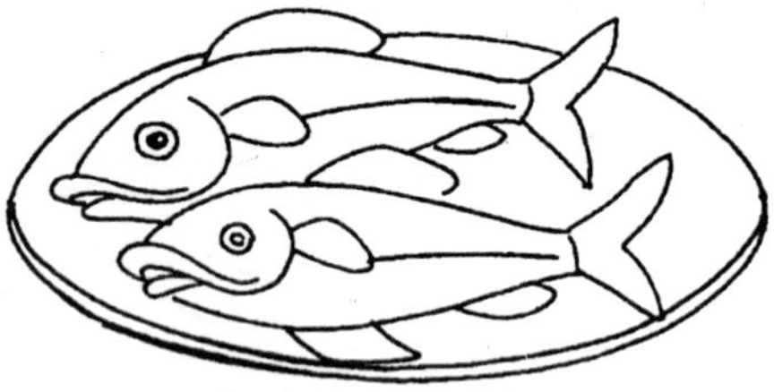 • • milk

 • • bun

Teacher/Parents : Ask the child to read the word aloud and recognise the picture.

Food

Fill in the blanks with the missing words.

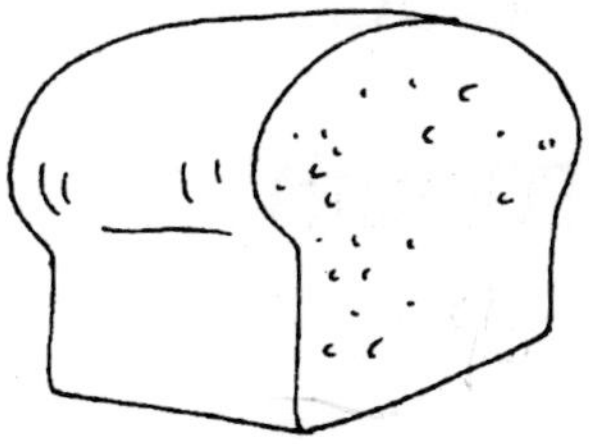 + 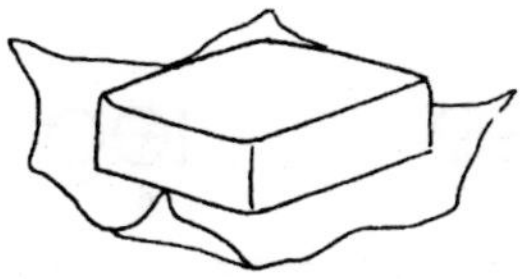 → 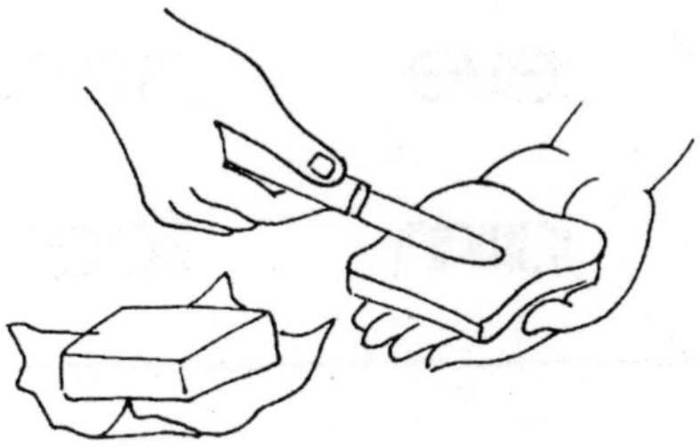

bread butter bread ______________

 + 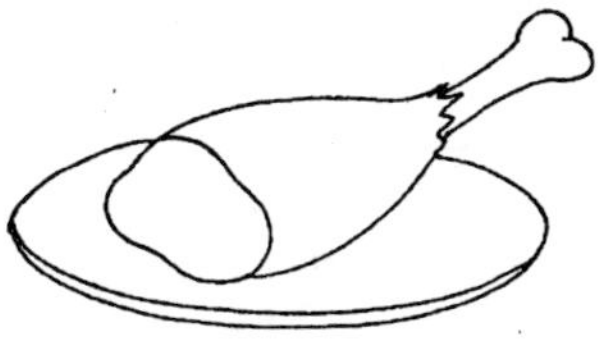 → 

rice chicken chicken ______________

 → 

eggs boiled ______________

 → 

cake birthday ______________

Teacher/Parents : Read the words aloud. Help the child to expand his/her knowledge of different types of a food item like boiled chicken, fried chicken, roasted chicken, etc.

My Body

Choose the correct word for each box.

eye	hand	ear	finger	head
arm	foot	nose	leg	mouth

Teacher/Parents : Help the child to identify the words.

My Body

Look at the picture carefully and circle the correct word.

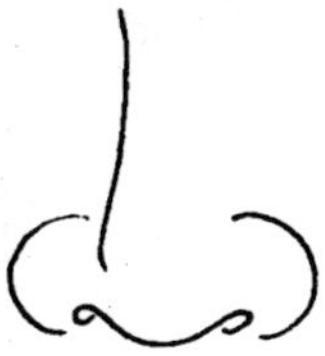	eyes	nose	ears
	foot	leg	hand
	ears	mouth	eyes
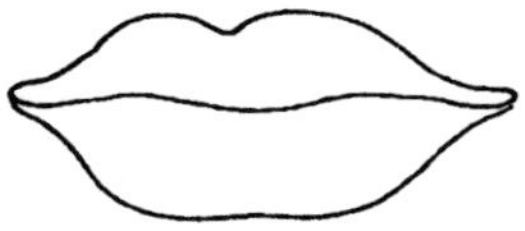	eyes	head	mouth
	head	hair	hand
	eyes	hand	ears

Teacher/Parents : Help the child to understand the different words.

Parts of the Body

Cat looks funny.
What is missing in the picture? Draw and write the name in the box.

______

Fill in the missing word.

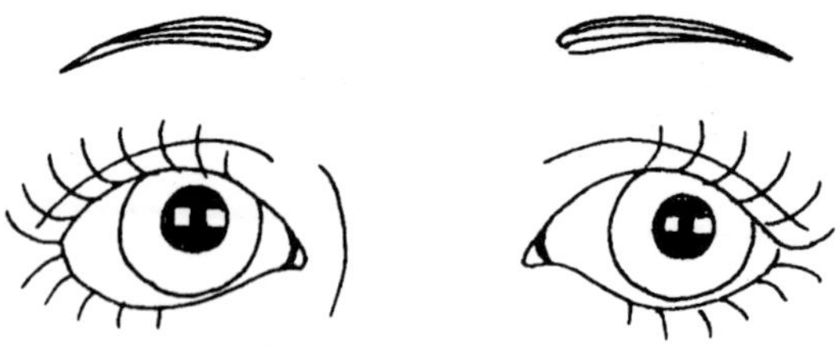

see

I ______________ with my eyes.

Teacher/Parents : What can you do with your eyes? You can close, open, wink, peep, etc. What do you see with your closed eyes ? What do you see with your opened eyes ?

Parts of the Body

Dog looks funny.
What is missing ? Draw the missing parts.
Write its name in the box.

What do you do with your ears ?
Fill in the blank with the missing word.

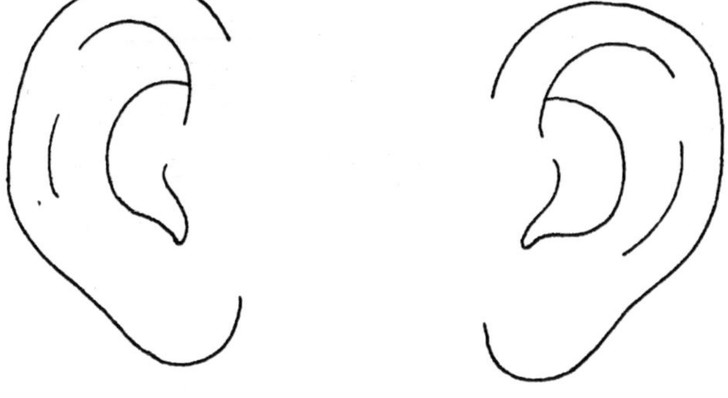

hear

I ________________ with my ears.

Teacher/Parents : What can you hear with your ears ? People talking, horn, music, noise, etc.

Look at the rabbit. Rabbit is looking funny.
What is missing on the rabbit's face?
Draw and write the name of missing part.

What do you do with your nose?
Fill in the missing word.

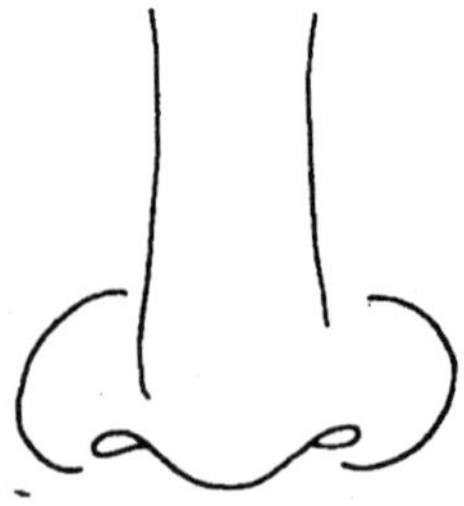

smell

I ____________________ with my nose.

Teacher/Parents : Explain the meaning of 'smell', 'bad smell' and 'good smell'. Ask the child to name some things, which smell good.

Parts of the Body

Lion looks funny.
Draw and name the missing part.

______

What do you do with your mouth?
Fill in the blanks with the missing words.

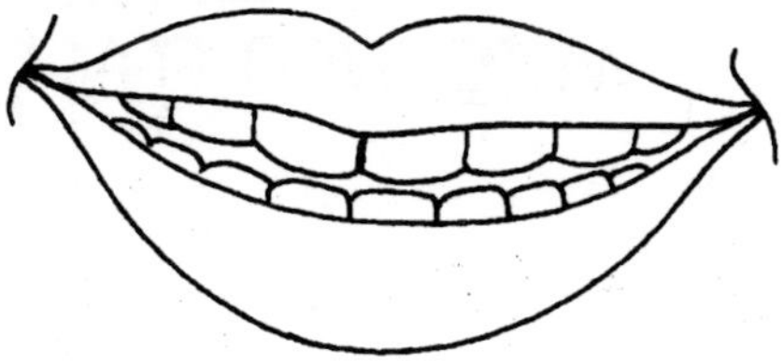

eat
drink

I ______________ with my mouth.

I ______________ with my mouth.

Teacher/Parents : Besides eating and drinking, what else can we do with our mouth? What other part of mouth helps us in talking?

Parts of the Body

Colour the hands.
What do you do with your hands?

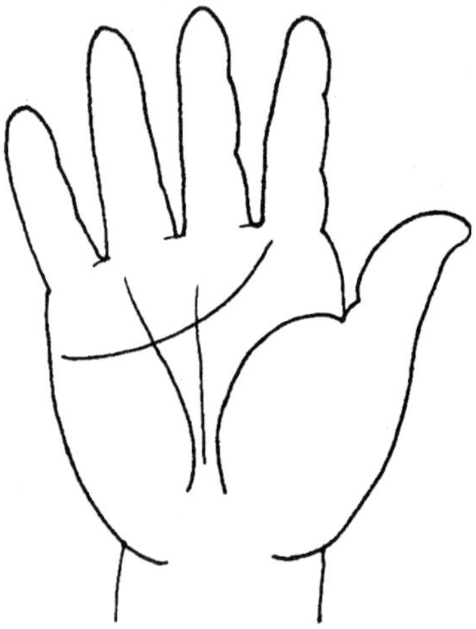

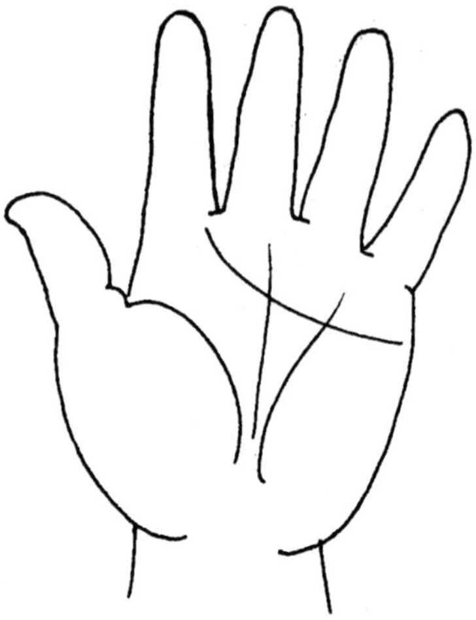

Draw lines to match the pictures with the sentences.

• • I carry my bag.

• • I write with my hand.

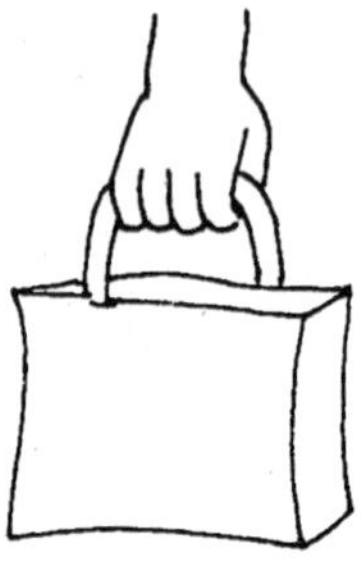

• • I clap with my hands.

Teacher/Parents : Ask the child to read and understand the sentences and then match each of them with appropriate picture.

Parts of the Body

What do you do with your legs ?
Match the pictures with the correct sentences.

I run with my legs.

I jump with my legs.

I walk with my legs.

I pedal with my legs

Teacher/Parents : Ask the child to identify the various parts of the leg : foot, toe, knee, ankle.

Parts of the Body

Join the animals with their legs.

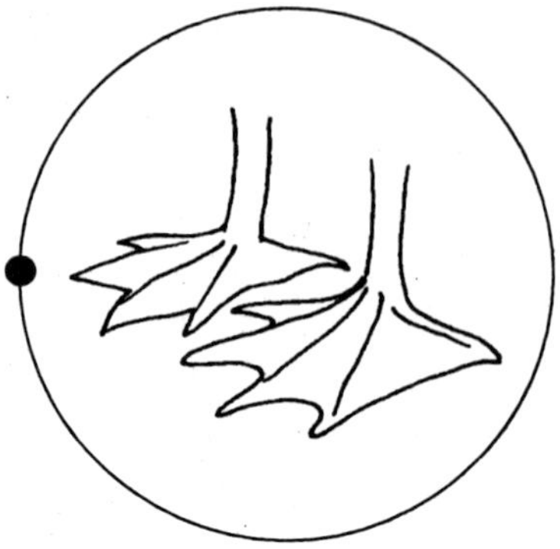

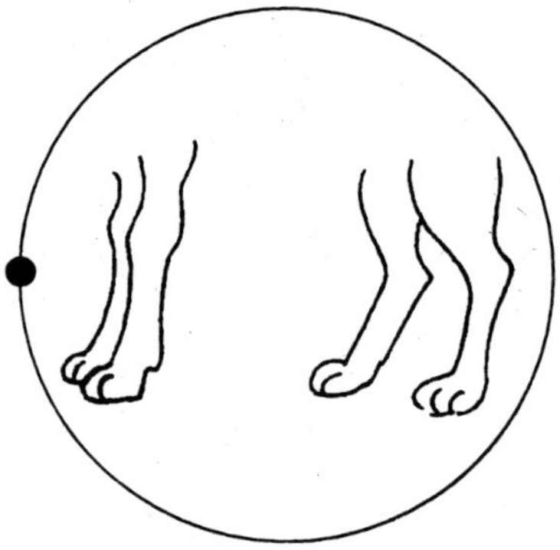

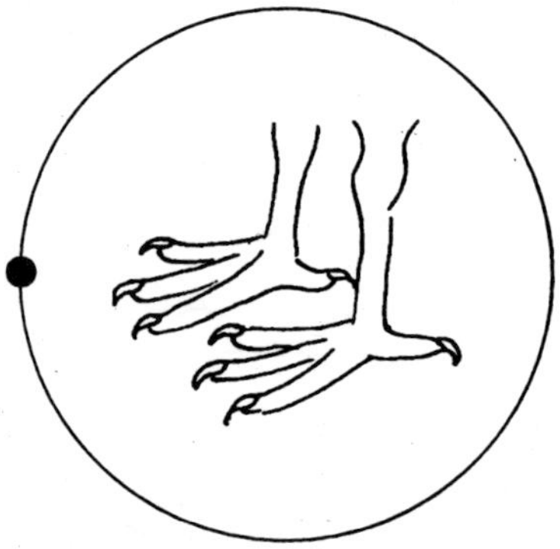

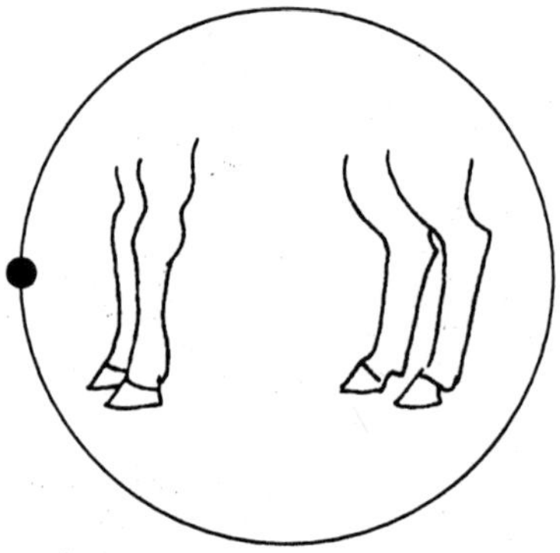

Teacher/Parents : Explain the child that how different animals use their legs in different ways like to scratch, to swim, etc.

My Animal Friends

Put a tick ☑ on the correct word.

	pig
	cow
	goat

	goat
	camel
	horse

	sheep
	goat
	pig

	duck
	goose
	hen

	sheep
	pig
	goat

Teacher/Parents : Help the child to identify the words.

Animals

Circle the correct animal.

Teacher/Parents : Help the child to identify and give names to the animals.

Animals

Here are some animal friends.
Fill in the blanks with 'horse', 'goat', 'rabbit', 'camel', 'cow' or 'donkey'.

This is a ____________________ .

This is a ____________________ .

This is a ____________________ .

This is a ____________________ .

This is a ____________________

This is a ____________________ .

Teacher/Parents : Help the child to name the animals. Discuss their characteristics.

Toys

Julie and John have many toys in their room.
Colour these toys and write their names in the boxes.

______ ______ ______

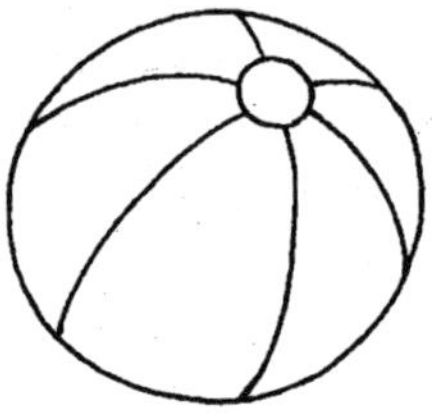

______ ______ ______

______

ball	doll	boat	car
train	teddy bear		helicopter

Teacher/Parents : Help the child to identify the toys.

Toys

Draw lines to match the pictures with correct words.

• gun

• kite

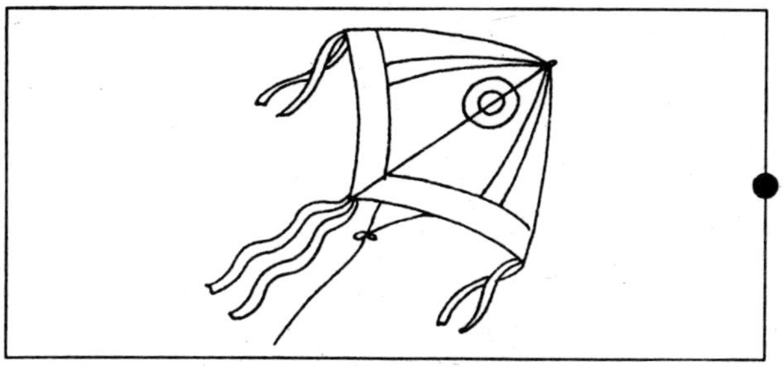

• ball

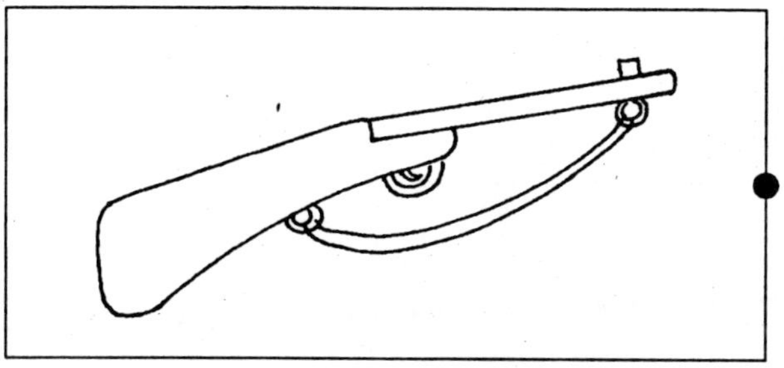

• car

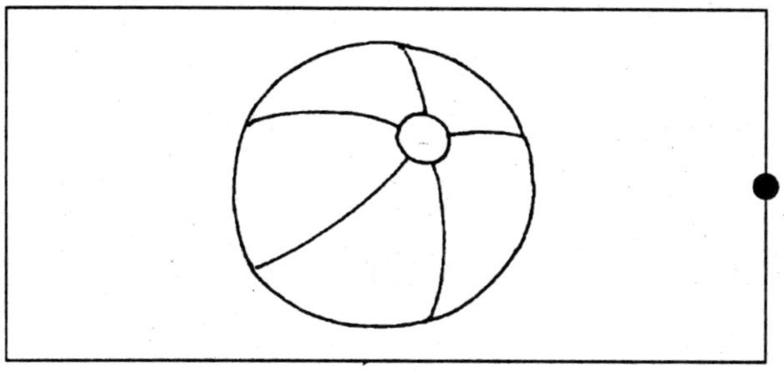

• doll

Teacher/Parents : Read the words aloud. Ask the child to identify the pictures.

At the Playground

Look at the pictures carefully. Name the things.
Draw lines to join each picture to the correct word.

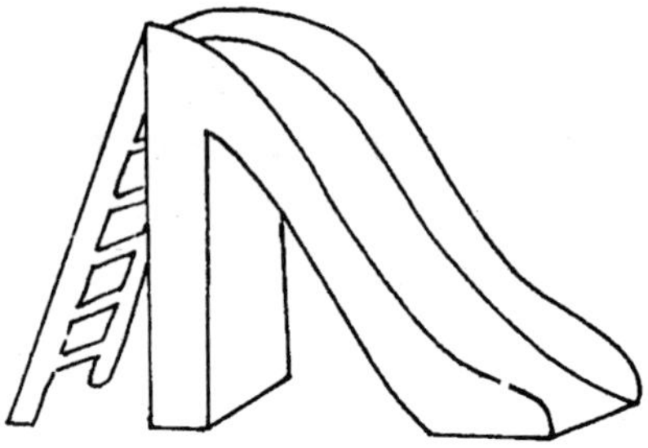

slide

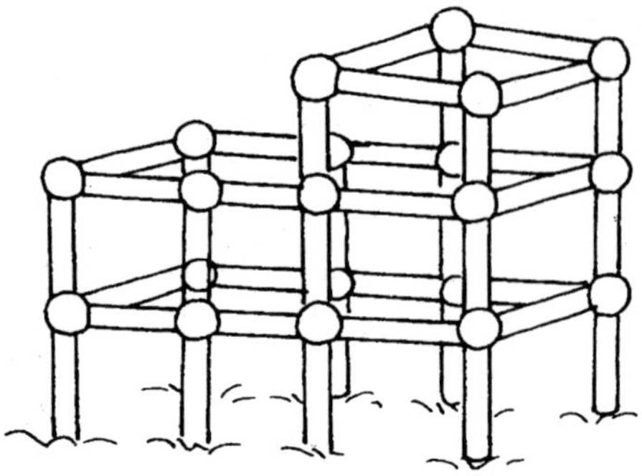

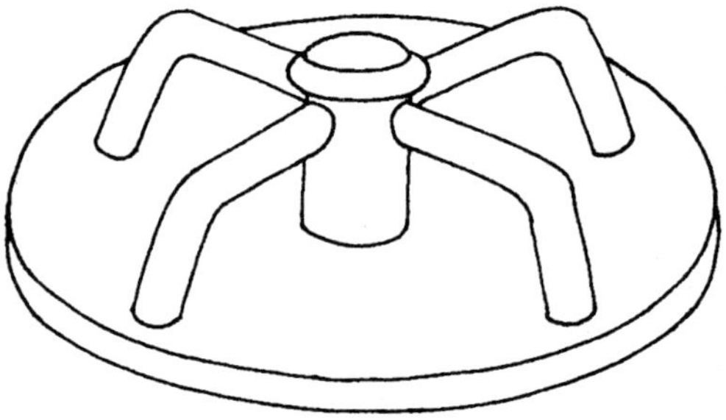

swing

see-saw

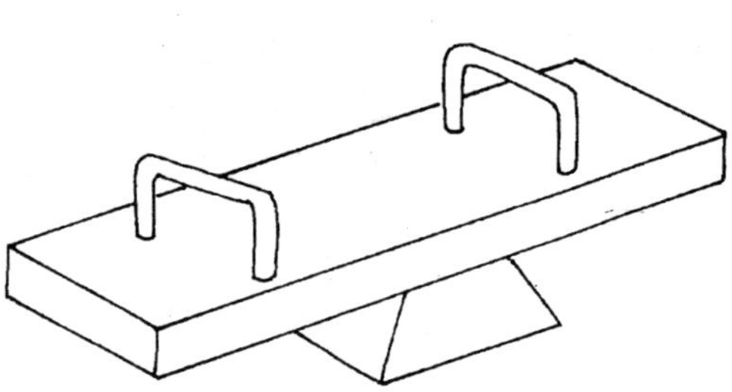

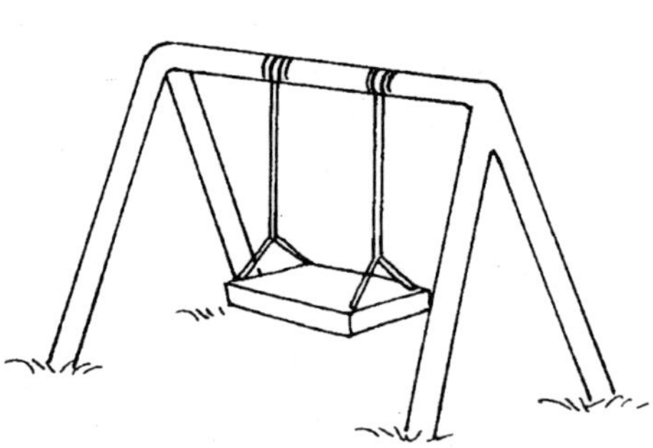

roundabout

jungle gym

Teacher/Parents : Pointing at the picture read the word aloud.

At the Playground

Colour the apples red which give the correct answers.

- slide
- swing
- see-saw

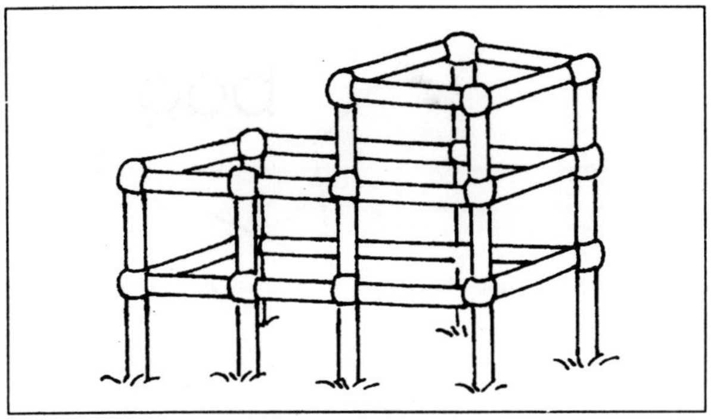

- jungle
- jump
- jungle gym

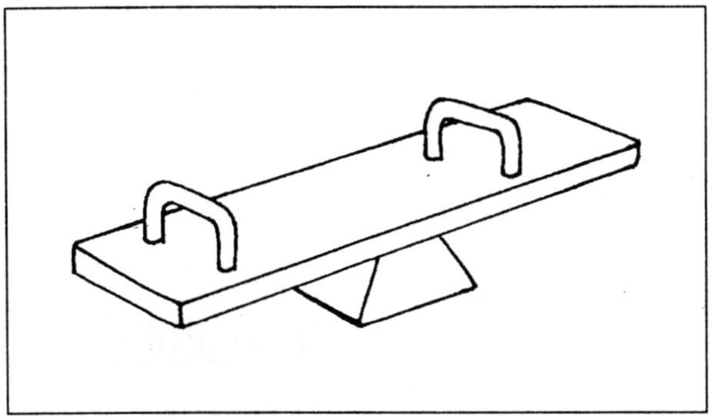

- sand
- seaside
- see-saw

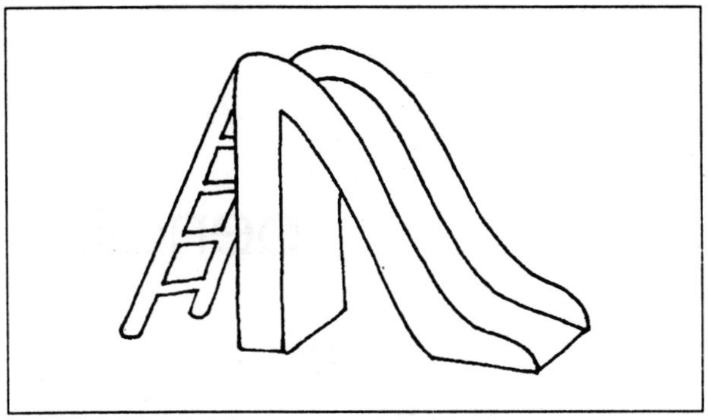

- slide
- swing
- sun

Teacher/Parents : Read the words aloud. Help the child to pronounce correctly so as to distinguish the words.

In the Classroom

Draw lines to match the pictures with the words.

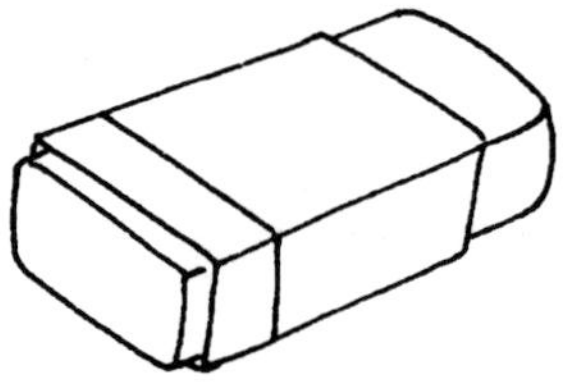

ruler

bag

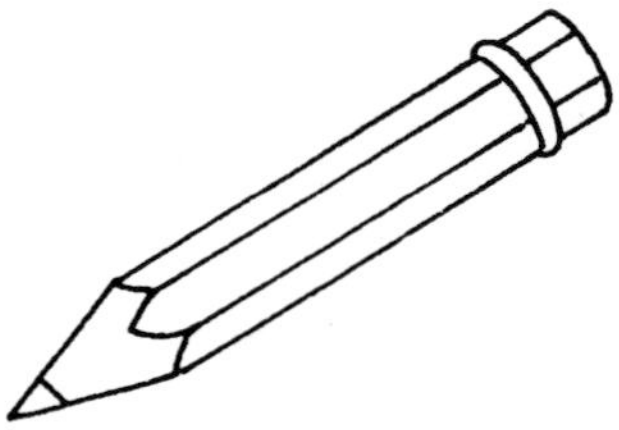

book

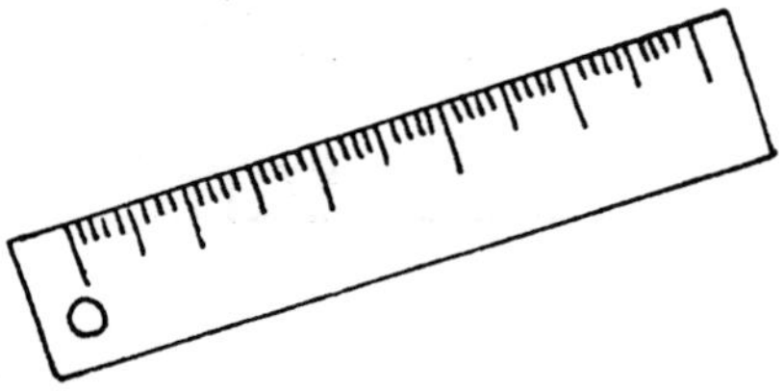

eraser

pencil

Teacher/Parents : Read each word aloud and help the child to match the word to the correct picture.

In the Classroom

Tony has many things in his school bag.

He has an ________________ .

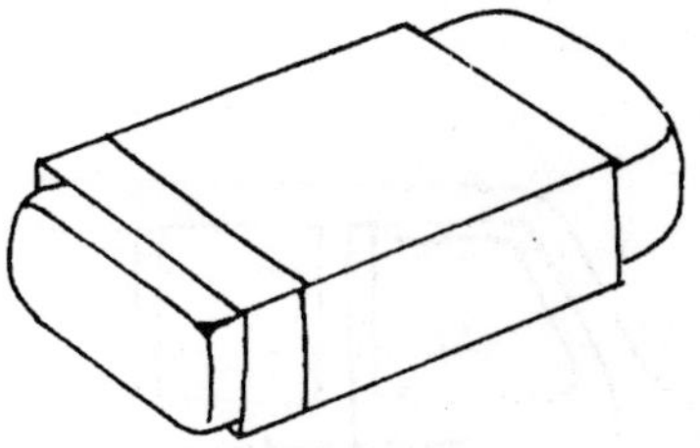

He has a ________________ .

He has many ________________ .

He has a ________________ .

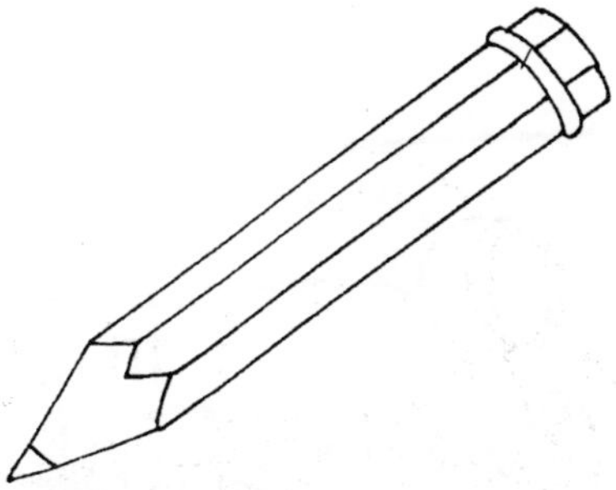

book	crayons	pencil	eraser

Teacher/Parents : Help the child to pick out the correct word and fill in the blank.

On the Road

Here are some vehicles. They are named wrongly.
Write the correct names in the boxes.

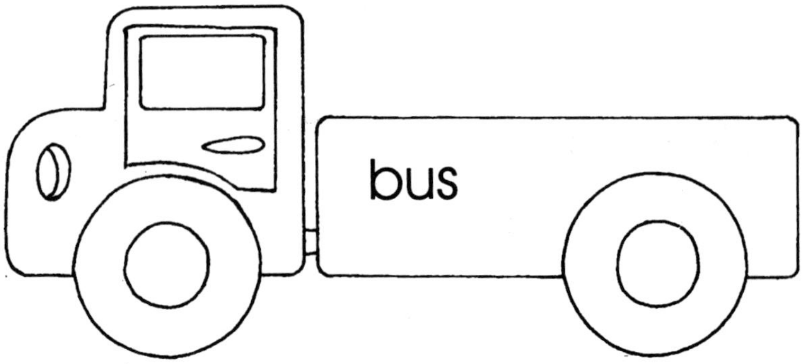

Teacher/Parents : Read each word aloud and ask the child to identify the picture.

On the Road

Colour the sign 'STOP' red.
Put a cross ☒ on the wrong picture.

Teacher/Parents : Discuss the importance of traffic signs on the road.

On the Road

Colour the sign 'GO' green.
Put a cross ☒ on the wrong picture.

Goodnight

This is Mona's bedroom.
Look for these objects and write their names in the boxes.

bed	story book	table
lamp	night-suit	pillow

Teacher/Parents : Read the words aloud. Help the child look for objects in the picture.

Big and Small

Colour the **elephant**.

The  is **big**.

Colour the **ant**.

The 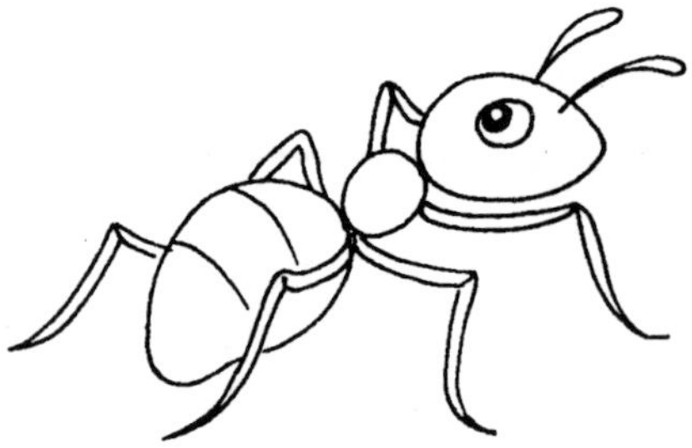 is **small**.

Teacher/Parents : Help the child to make out the difference between some other 'big-small' objects.

Big and Small

Which animals are small? Circle them.
Can you name the small animals?

Tall and Short

Colour the **giraffe**.

The  is **tall.**

Colour the **rabbit**.

The  is **short.**

Teacher/Parents : Help the child to identify the words 'tall and short'.

Tall and Short

Which objects are tall? Can you name them?

Up and Down

Colour the aeroplanes.

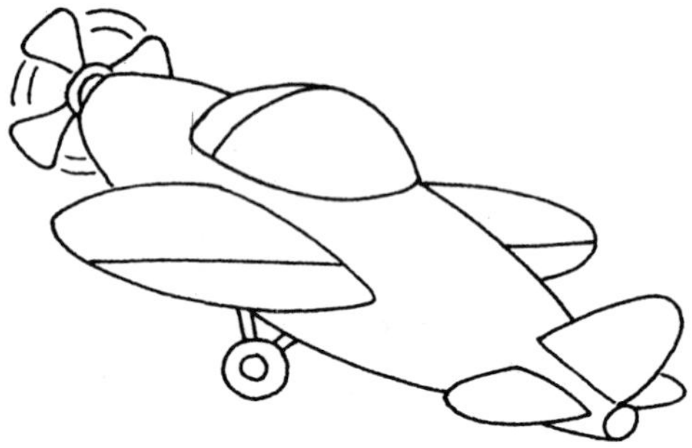

The aeroplane is going **up**.

The aeroplane is coming **down**.

Teacher/Parents : Read the sentences aloud. Help the child to identify the words 'up and down'.

Up and Down

Who is up ?
Who is down ?

Gopal is ____________________

Mona is ____________________

Happy and Sad

Colour the pictures.

Happy

Sad

Teacher/Parents : Help the child to recognize and identify the words 'happy and sad'.

Happy and Sad

Draw lines to match the feelings.

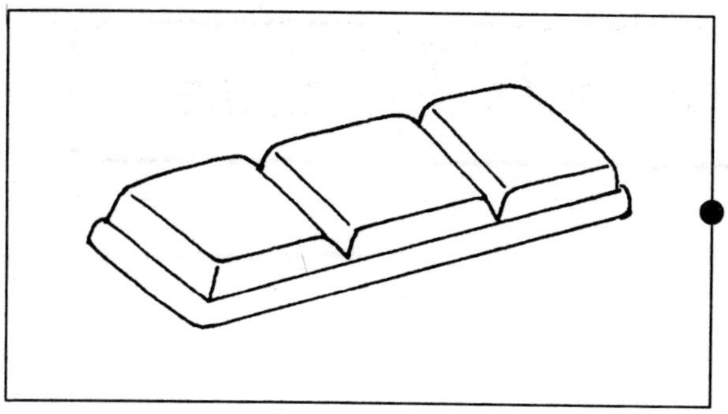

Teacher/Parents : Encourage the child with more use of the words 'happy and sad'.

People I Know

Look at the pictures carefully.
Write the correct word in each box.

teacher	doctor	postman	nurse

Teacher/Parents : Help the child to identify the pictures first and then write the correct name of each picture.

People I Know

Look at the pictures carefully.
Write the correct word in each box.

policeman	dentist	soldier	fireman

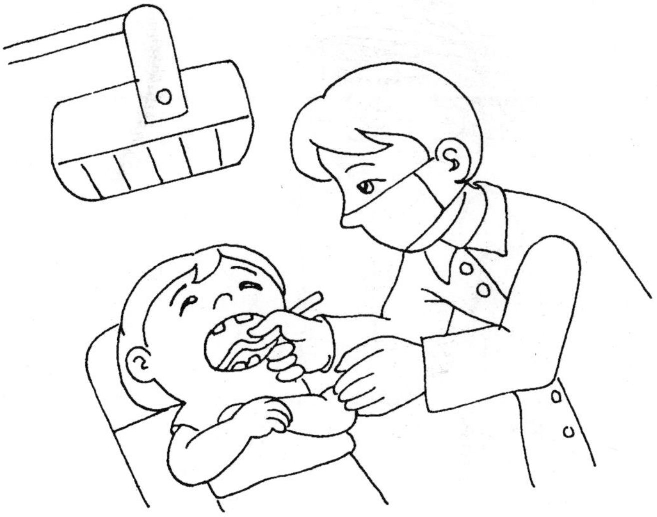

People I Know

Pick out the correct word and write in the box.

cobbler	milkman	barber	washerman

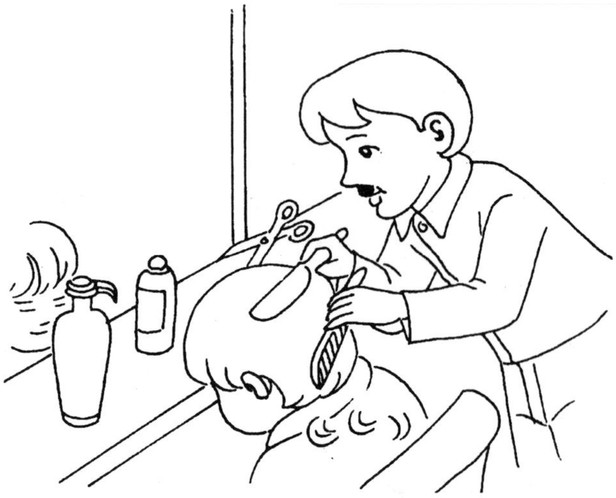

People I Know

Look at the pictures. Read the sentences carefully.
Draw line to match each picture to the correct sentence.

- He looks after sick people.

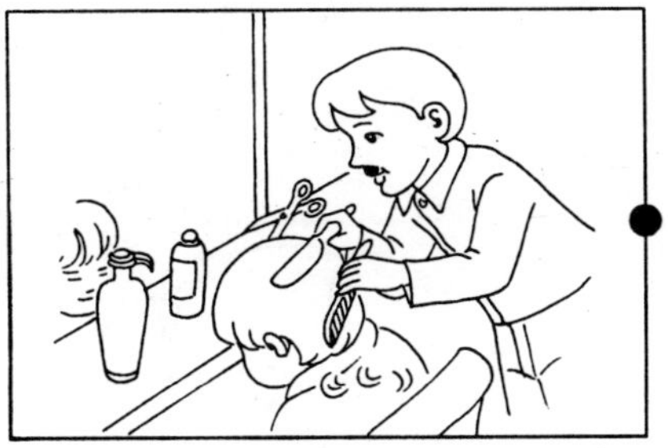

- He cuts my hair.

- He protects our country.

- He mends my shoes.

- He brings letters to our house.

Teacher/Parents : Read the sentences. Help the child to match each sentence with the correct picture.

Action Words

Draw lines to match the pictures with the words.

eat

drink

brush

wash

walk

run

Teacher/Parents : Help the child to recognize the words. Talk about the actions in the picture.

Action Words

Draw lines to match the pictures with the words.

- climb
- jump
- sit
- stand
- read
- write

Teacher/Parents : Read the words aloud and discuss about the actions.

Action Words

Trace and then match the words.

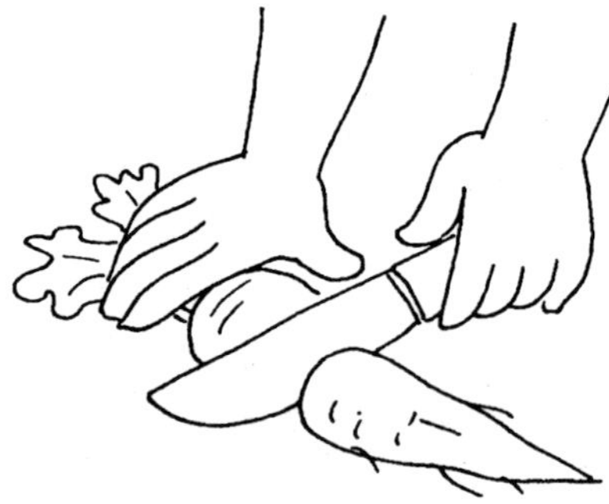

- comb
- paint
- sleep
- cut

Teacher/Parents : Help the child to match each word with the correct action.

Action Words

What is little Rohan doing?
Put a tick ☑ on the correct action/doing word.

- [ ] wash
- [ ] drink
- [ ] brush

- [ ] sit
- [ ] stand
- [ ] sleep

- [ ] run
- [ ] jump
- [ ] swim

- [ ] run
- [ ] walk
- [ ] jump

- [ ] climb
- [ ] jump
- [ ] run

Position Words

Fill in the blanks with the missing words.

The lamp is ________________ the table.

The fruit basket is ________________ the table.

The puppy is ________________ the table.

Teacher/Parents : Read the words and sentences. Encourage the child with the use of position words giving more examples.

Position Words

Fill in the blanks with the missing words.

The lion is ________________ the den.

The lion is ________________ of the den.

Position Words

Fill in the blanks with 'behind', 'up' and 'down'.

The monkey is ____________________ on the tree.

The dog is ____________________ the tree.

The cat is coming ____________________ the tree.

Position Words

Look at the pictures carefully. Circle the correct position words.

The butterfly is flying over / under the flower.

The cat is over / under the table.

The puppy is in / out of the basket.

The crow is on / over the cow.

The parrot is in / out the cage.

Word Knowledge

Fill in the blanks with the correct words.

I ______________ my hair with a **hair-brush.**

hair-brush

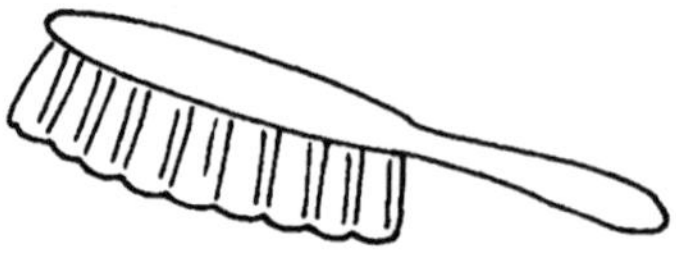

brush

I ______________ a **story-book.**

story-book

read

I ______________ a picture with a **pencil.**

pencil

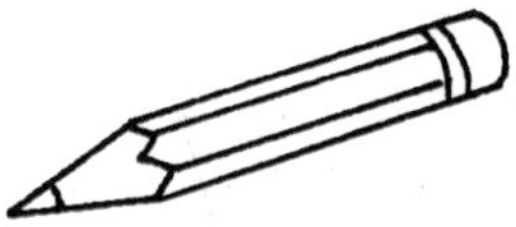

draw

I ______________ vegetables with a **knife.**

knife

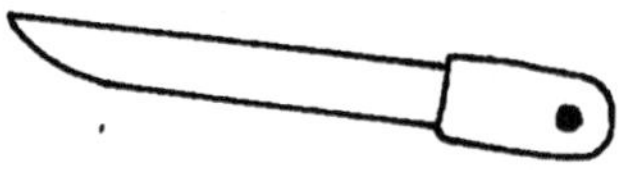

cut

I ______________ my hair with a **comb.**

comb

comb

Teacher/Parents : Help the child to identify the words. Read the sentences.

I can __________ an **apple** daily.

apple

eat

I can __________ my teeth with a **tooth-brush**.

tooth-brush

brush

I can __________ a glass of **milk**.

milk

drink

I can __________ **football**.

football

play

I can __________ a **kite**.

kite

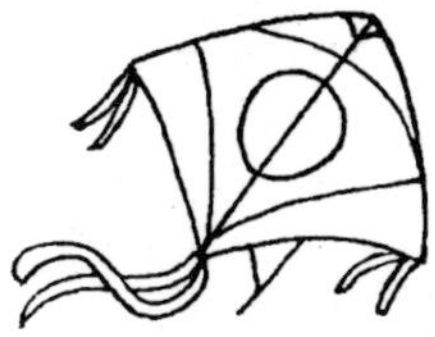

fly

Word Knowledge

How do I feel?
Choose the correct words and circle them.

I am happy / sad.

I am happy / sad.

I am happy / sad.

I am happy / sad.

Word Knowledge

Trace and read the words.

hot   cold

Circle the things that make you cool.

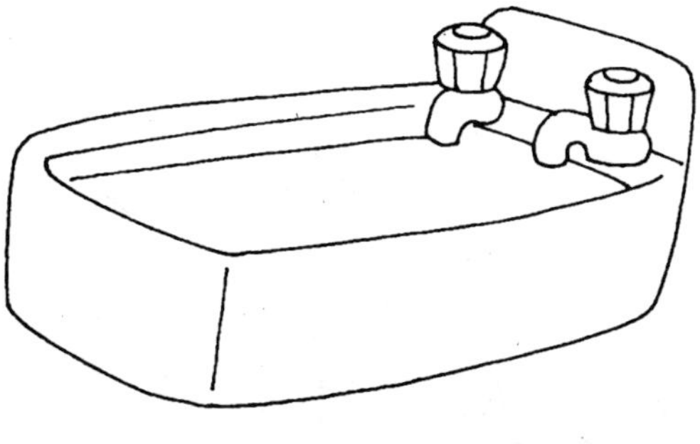

Word Knowledge

How do parents feel?
Colour the picture that will make father **angry**.

Colour the picture that will make mother **angry**.